A WORLD OF GODS

ROAR!

Ancient GREEK Gods

by Eliza Nodes

BEARPORT PUBLISHING

Roar! Books, an imprint of Bearport Publishing by FlutterBee

Credits

All images are courtesy of Shutterstock.com, unless otherwise stated. Recurring – C_Atta, Macrovector, Anna Timoshenko; Cover, © NCKAHDE, Jasonsimsjs; 4–5, © Viacheslav Lopatin, Lyubena Stoimenova; 6–7, © turtix; 8–9, © public domain, via Wikimedia Commons, Gilmanshin; 10–11, © Kevin Ruck; 12–13, © sweet marshmallow, Zwiebackesser; 14–15, © Guillaume Angleraud; 16–17, © rawf8, michaeladesign; 18–19, © zedspider; 20–21, © Morphart Creation; 22–23, © Andrij Vatsyk; 24–25, © public domain, via Wikimedia Commons; 26–27, © Gilmanshin; 28–29, © KrimKate, Aleksandr Simonov; 30, © yiannisscheidt; 31, © Yueh Chiang.

Bearport Publishing Company Product Development Team

Kayla Eggert, Theresa Emminizer, Kim Jones, Allison Juda, Cole Nelson, Naomi Reich, Steve Scheluchin, Tiana Tran

Library of Congress Cataloging-in-Publication Data is available at www.loc.gov or upon request from the publisher.

ISBN: 979-8-89577-852-4 (hardcover)
ISBN: 979-8-89577-856-2 (paperback)
ISBN: 979-8-89577-860-9 (ebook)

For more information, write to Bearport Publishing, 3500 American Blvd W, Suite 150, Bloomington, MN 55431. Printed in the United States of America.

CONTENTS

ANCIENT GREECE

The ancient Greek civilization lasted from about 700 **BCE** to around 323 BCE. Its people worshipped a powerful group of gods.

The Greeks believed that Gaia, the Earth goddess, created the Titans. These were mighty rulers that lived on Mount Othrys. Zeus was the son of Titans.

Zeus fought a war to overthrow the Titans and became king of the gods. He moved their home to Mount Olympus. These new gods called themselves Olympians.

Modern-day Greece is much smaller than the ancient Greek civilization, which was spread throughout the Mediterranean.

There were 12 Olympian gods. Each had their own powers, special symbols, and places of worship.

ZEUS

Zeus ruled over everyone and everything. He was also the god of a few specific things. He ruled the sky and fierce weather.

Zeus was also the god of hospitality, or the kind treatment of guests and strangers. This was an important part of life in ancient Greece. The Greeks believed that people who were not good hosts would be punished by Zeus!

Zeus married the goddess Hera. The king of gods also had many children.

The main place to worship Zeus was a temple in Olympia. It was built around 460 BCE. The temple had a huge statue of Zeus.

The ancient Greeks created the Olympic Games to honor Zeus.

THE RISE OF ZEUS

Zeus's parents were Titans named Cronus and Rhea. One day, Cronus heard a **prophecy**. It said that one of his children would overthrow him and take his power. Cronus didn't want the prophecy to come true. To stop it, he swallowed his own children!

Cronus swallowed five of his six children. To save her last child, Rhea had to act fast. She tricked Cronus into swallowing a stone instead of baby Zeus.

Rhea raised Zeus in secret on the island of Crete. When Zeus grew up, he fought and defeated Cronus and freed his swallowed siblings. Zeus was then named king of the gods.

ATHENA

Athena was one of Zeus's daughters. She was his favorite child!

Athena was the goddess of wisdom and war. She found clever ways to solve problems peacefully rather than using violence.

Athena is often shown wearing armor, as if she is dressed for battle. She sometimes has an owl beside her. This is a symbol of her great wisdom. Snakes and olive trees are symbols of Athena, too.

The Parthenon was built around 447 BCE and is still standing today!

The city of Athens was named for Athena. A huge temple was built there to honor her. It was called the Parthenon.

HOW ATHENS GOT ITS NAME

The ancient Greeks believed that a city needed a powerful god as its **patron**. Athena and Poseidon both wanted the role. Zeus held a contest for the townspeople to choose between the two gods.

Poseidon and Athena used their powers to create gifts for the city. Poseidon made a fountain of seawater. Athena grew an olive tree. The people could eat the olives from Athena's tree but couldn't drink Poseidon's salty water.

So, the people chose Athena as their patron. They named the city Athens in her honor.

ARTEMIS

Artemis was another one of Zeus's daughters. She was the goddess of hunting.

Artemis is often shown holding a bow and arrow. A hunting dog or deer is usually by her side.

The largest **sanctuary** honoring Artemis is called the Artemision. Its remains can be found in modern-day Turkey.

REMAINS OF THE ARTEMISION

In addition to being a hunter, Artemis was a midwife. This is someone who helps people give birth. Artemis helped her own mother give birth to her twin brother!

DELIVERING APOLLO

Artemis and Apollo's mother was named Leto. Zeus's wife, Hera, was jealous of Leto. So, Leto hid on the island of Delos to stay safe from Hera.

Leto gave birth to Artemis on the island. However, she soon realized that she was having twins.

Unfortunately, the second baby would not come out. Some say Hera made this happen. Others say the baby was just stuck. Either way, Leto was in a lot of pain.

Even though Artemis had just been born, she helped her mother deliver her baby brother, Apollo.

APOLLO

Apollo was the god of light, music, and poetry. He played a small stringed instrument called a lyre. A lyre is a bit like a harp.

The ancient Greeks believed that if they prayed to Apollo for guidance, he might send them a special message through a person called an oracle.

Apollo's oracle lived in a place called Delphi. People came from all over Greece to ask the oracle questions.

The oracle of Delphi was known for giving confusing but truthful prophecies.

KILLING THE PYTHON

Hera was very angry when she heard that Apollo and Artemis had been born.

She sent the giant snake Python to kill Apollo. The young god heard about Hera's plot. He asked Hephaestus, the god of fire, to make him a weapon. He gave Apollo a golden bow and arrow.

Apollo tracked Python to his cave, and the two fought. It was a tough battle, but Apollo eventually killed Python.

The ancient Greeks celebrated Apollo's victory over Python. Every four years, they held a series of athletic and musical **competitions** called the Pythian Games.

HERMES

Hermes was the son of Zeus and Maia. He was the god of thieves and travelers. This god was known for being a clever trickster.

Hermes delivered messages between the gods. Zeus often sent him to give orders to other gods.

Hermes was extremely quick. He wore a pair of winged sandals that helped speed him on his way to deliver messages.

Hermes also worked for Hades, the god of the dead. He collected the souls of the dead and took them to the underworld.

The ancient Greeks believed everyone went to the underworld after they died.

A THIEF AND A TRICKSTER

Hermes was loved by all the gods. Although he liked to play tricks, his charm often got him out of trouble!

When Hermes was young, he found a herd of white cows that belonged to Apollo. Hermes took the cows back to the cave where he lived.

When Apollo heard that his cows had been stolen, he became very angry. He hunted down Hermes and found him in his cave.

Hermes knew that Apollo loved music. To win over the angry god, he gave Apollo a beautiful lyre that he had made from a tortoise shell.

APHRODITE

Aphrodite was famously beautiful. She was the goddess of love and **fertility**.

People prayed to Aphrodite when they wanted children. They made **sacrifices** to her in the form of things that smell sweet, such as flowers and **incense**.

The ancient Greeks held a special celebration to honor the goddess of love and her powers. They called the event Aphrodisia.

Roses, doves, and seashells were some of Aphrodite's symbols.

Aphrodite was often shown with seashells because of her unique birth story. She had special ties to the ocean and to sea travelers.

APHRODITE'S BIRTH

Aphrodite's birth was different from those of other gods. She wasn't born from a mother. Instead, she came from the sea itself!

A sickle is a curved blade with a handle.

The story goes that Aphrodite was born while Zeus was battling Ouranos, the god of the sky. Zeus slashed at Ouranos with a sickle, cutting him and sending part of the god into the sea!

The sea bubbled up into foam. Then, a large seashell appeared. Inside the seashell was a woman. It was Aphrodite!

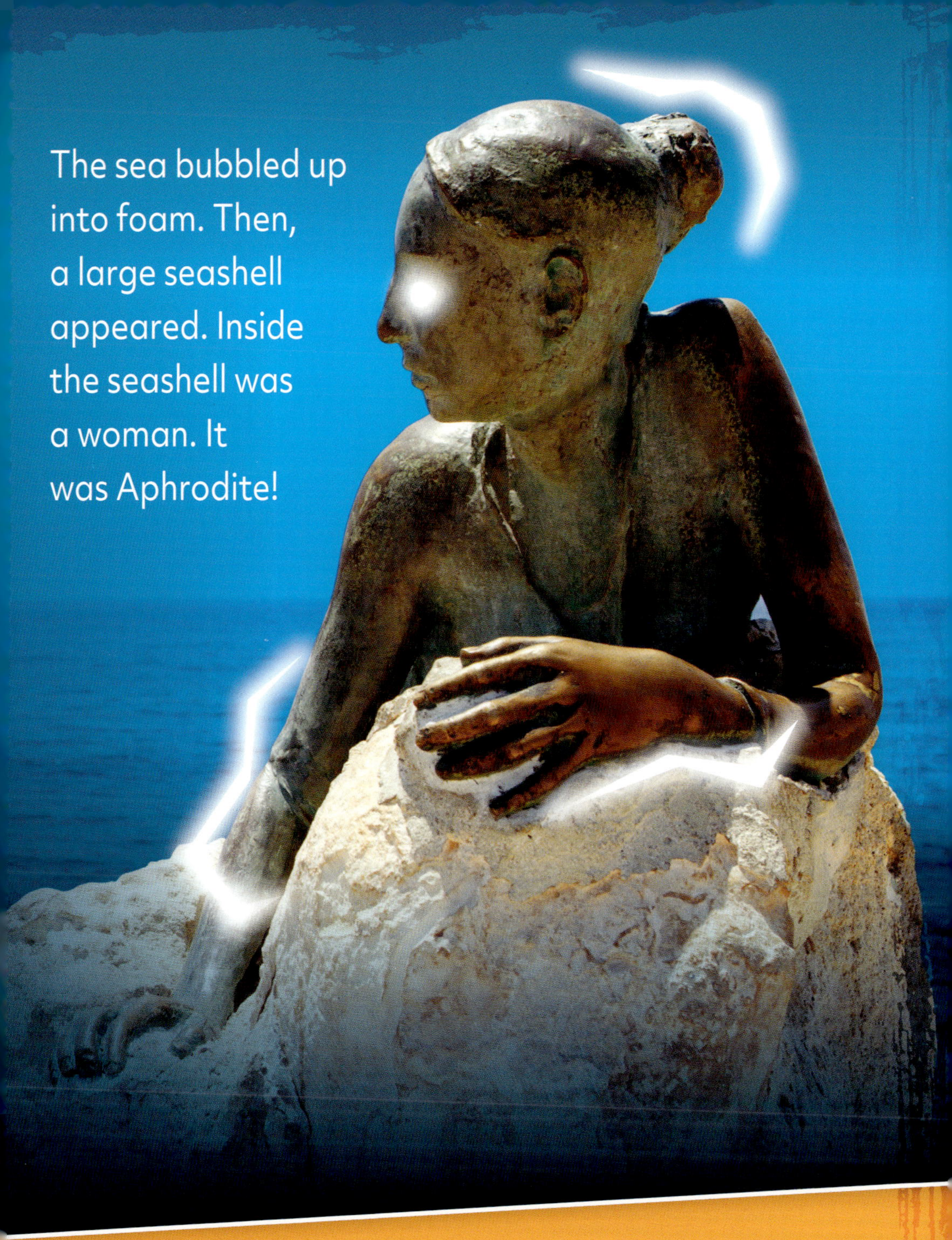

The seashell washed up on an island. Aphrodite stepped out and walked on land for the first time.

THE LEGENDS LIVE ON

Worship of the Greek gods faded with the rise of the Roman Empire. But stories of the gods have stood the test of time.

Even after thousands of years, people are still captivated by Greek legends. These mythical heroes have inspired artwork, poetry, books, movies, and even video games. Though the ancient Greeks are gone, their gods live on!

GLOSSARY

BCE Before Common Era, the time before the year 1

competitions contests between two teams or rivals to decide a winner

fertility the ability to have babies

incense something that's burned to make a sweet smell

patron someone who supports another person, activity, or cause

prophecy a prediction or statement about something that will happen in the future

sacrifices offerings made to a god

sanctuary a place where people pray and make sacrifices to a particular god

INDEX

READ MORE

Leatherland, Noah. *Life in Ancient Greece (Baffling Behavior in the Past)*. Minneapolis: Bearport Publishing, 2025.

Sheldon-Dean, Hannah. *Who's Who? Greek Mythology: The Gods, Heroes, and Monsters of Legend*. Nashville: Applesauce Press, 2024.

LEARN MORE ONLINE

1. Go to **FactSurfer.com** or scan the QR code below.
2. Enter "**Ancient Greek Gods**" into the search box.
3. Click on the cover of this book to see a list of websites.